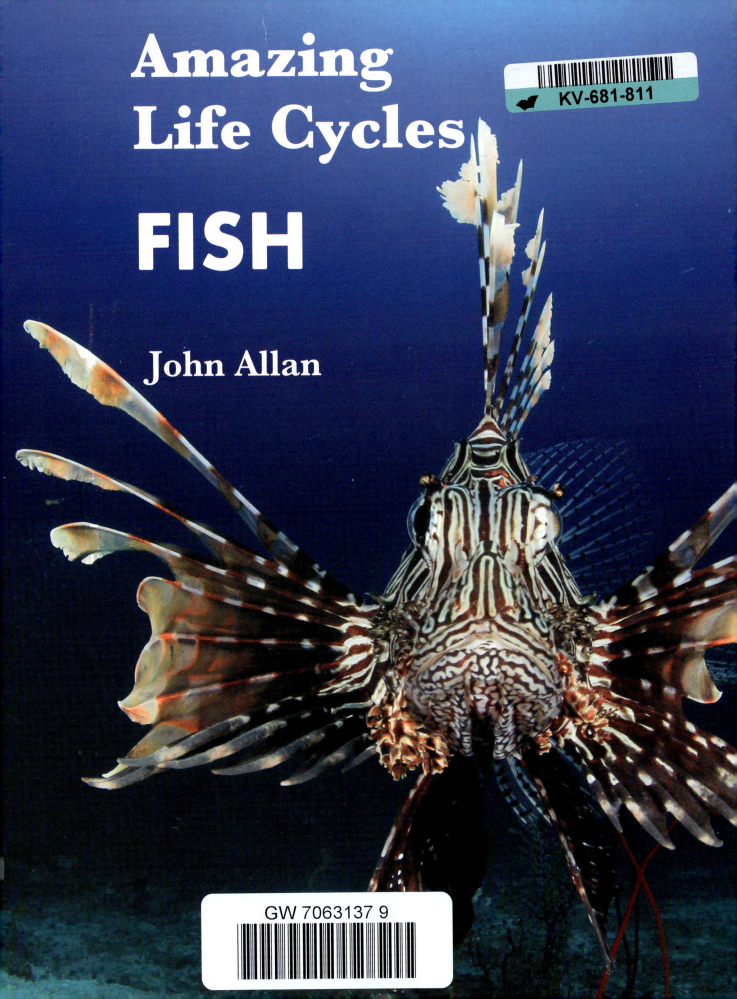

Amazing Life Cycles

FISH

John Allan

Great white sharks are one of the largest fish in our seas and live for up to 30 years.

Contents

ISBN 978-1-913077-03-7

Copyright © 2020 Hungry Tomato Ltd
First published in Great Britain in 2020 by
Hungry Tomato Ltd, The Old Bakery Studios, Blewetts Wharf,
Malpas Road, Truro, Cornwall, TR1 1QH, UK

Printed and bound in China

Words that look **bold like this** are in the glossary.

What is a fish?

Fish are covered in scales that help to protect them.

A fish is an animal that lives in water. It usually has fins and **scales**. A fish can breathe underwater using body parts called **gills**. The gills take **oxygen** out of the water and pass it into the fish's body.

Fish use their fins and tail to move through the water.

Fin

Tail

Fin

Gill cover

Some fish live alone. Others live in big groups called shoals. A shoal can have hundreds or thousands of fish.

Most fish **reproduce** by laying eggs. The eggs are very small and soft. The female fish usually lays hundreds of eggs in one go.

These fish eggs have been attached to an underwater rock by a female fish.

A great white shark.

Sharks are a type of fish. Some sharks, such as the great white shark, give birth to live babies called pups.

AMAZING FISH FACT
When great white shark pups are born they are over one metre long and have sharp teeth, ready for hunting!

Fish habitats

A habitat is the place where a plant or an animal lives. The ocean is a habitat, so are rivers and lakes. Many fish live in the ocean, which is **saltwater.** *Other types of fish live in* **freshwater** *ponds or streams.*

Blue tang fish live in holes and cracks on coral reefs.

Fish live in all of the world's oceans.

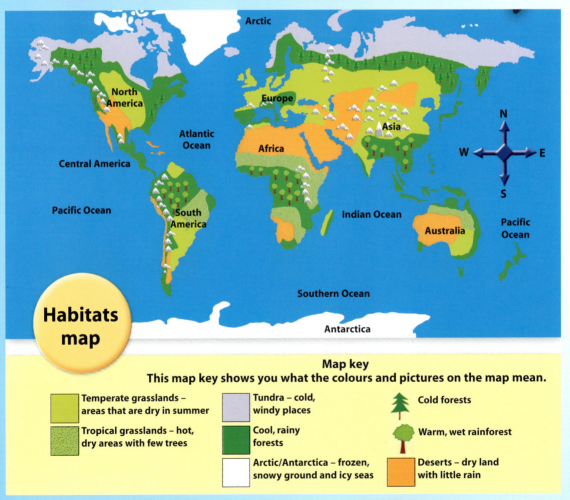

Arctic

North America

Europe

Asia

Atlantic Ocean

Africa

Central America

Pacific Ocean

South America

Indian Ocean

Australia

Pacific Ocean

Southern Ocean

Antarctica

N
W E
S

Habitats map

Map key
This map key shows you what the colours and pictures on the map mean.

Temperate grasslands – areas that are dry in summer

Tropical grasslands – hot, dry areas with few trees

Arctic/Antarctica – frozen, snowy ground and icy seas

Tundra – cold, windy places

Cool, rainy forests

Cold forests

Warm, wet rainforest

Deserts – dry land with little rain

Some of the most colourful fish live around **coral reefs.** These reefs grow near to the surface of the water in warm oceans.

Some strange looking fish live at the very bottom of deep oceans where it is cold and dark. There is very little food there.

The deepwater fangtooth fish (above) has a huge mouth that helps it catch any fish it can find—even if the fish is the same size as the fangtooth fish!

The mudskipper is a fish that lives in shallow muddy freshwater **swamps**. It spends most of its time out of water and can "walk" using its fins.

AMAZING FISH FACT
The fangtooth fish has huge eyes to help it see in the dark.

Ocean fish

Stonefish live on the ocean floor. They look just like stones and have a nasty sting!

Ocean fish can be just 3 cm long or enormous like the whale shark—the biggest fish in the world! Some ocean fish don't even look like fish, but more like seaweed or stones.

Whale shark

Many fish that live in coral reefs have bright colours or patterns that help keep them safe from **predators**, such as bigger fish.

AMAZING FISH FACT
The whale shark can grow to 15 metres long. It's not a hunter though. It only eats **plankton**.

The tomato clownfish lives on coral reefs hidden from predators among the stinging tentacles of **sea anemones**.

The clownfish's body is covered in a special slime. Scientists believe the slime protects the fish from the anemone's stings.

Sea anemone

Tomato clownfish

Pretend eye

This butterfly fish's black spot looks like an eye. A predator is not sure which end is the right end to attack.

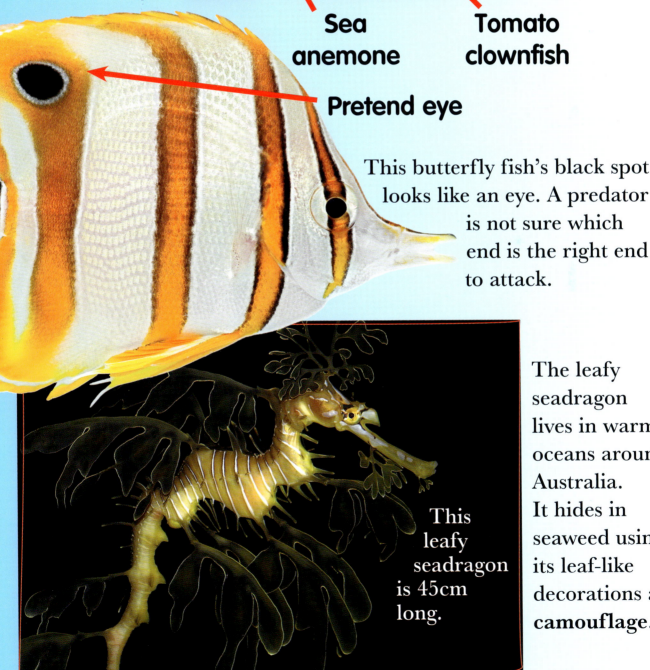

This leafy seadragon is 45cm long.

The leafy seadragon lives in warm oceans around Australia. It hides in seaweed using its leaf-like decorations as **camouflage**.

Freshwater fish

Perch live in rivers and lakes. Females lay 300,000 eggs at one time!

Some freshwater fish live in clear, flowing streams or rivers. Others live in ponds where the water is very still and where lots of weeds grow.

Piranhas live in freshwater rivers in South America

Piranhas are freshwater fish that eat other fish, insects, seeds, and fruit. But sometimes piranhas will eat larger animals!

Piranhas have razor-sharp teeth!

If the river dries up during a hot time of year, the piranhas are forced to live together in a small amount of water. If a large animal, such as a horse, steps into the water, the hungry piranhas will attack as a group!

Catfish use their whiskers, or barbels, to feel for food along the bottom of lakes and rivers.

Barbel

Catfish live in lakes and rivers. They eat fish, shellfish and any other small creatures they can find. They usually feed at night.

Mum meets dad

This is a pair of long-nosed butterfly fish. All butterfly fish pair for life.

Most fish reproduce every year. Some fish find a mate and stay together as a pair for life. Other fish have a new partner each year. Many fish mate with more than one partner in the same year.

Emperor angelfish live on coral

A male emperor angelfish lives with up to five female mates. If the male dies, one of the females turns into a male fish and becomes the leader of the group!

The angelfish pair in this photo are guarding their eggs.

Freshwater angelfish stay together as a pair for life. After mating, the female lays about 1,000 eggs on a leaf.

Eggs

Hammerhead sharks can live in shoals of over 500 sharks. The strongest female swims in the middle of the shoal.

When she is ready to mate, the strongest female starts shaking her head from side to side. This makes the other females swim to the edges of the shoal.

Now the strongest female is the center of attention and is sure to get a mate.

AMAZING FISH FACT
Sharks live in all the world's oceans. They have been around since before the dinosaurs!

What is a life cycle?

This is a pair of red flower horn fish. There are about 24,500 different types of fish.

A life cycle is all the different stages and changes that a plant or animal goes through in its life. The diagrams on these pages show examples of fish life cycles.

An adult male and female fish meet. Some fish make a nest.

1

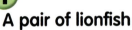
A pair of lionfish

The female fish lays her eggs. The male fish covers the eggs with a liquid from his body called sperm. Now the eggs are fertilized.

4

Baby fish with the father

FISH LIFE CYCLE
Many fish have a life cycle with these stages.

2

Fertilized fish eggs

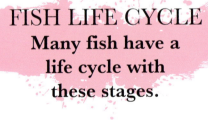

Baby fish called fry hatch from the eggs. The tiny babies take care of themselves. They have a yolk sack, which they use as food.

3

A pair of angelfish

Some fish guard their eggs. Others leave them to hatch on their own.

1 A pair of white top reef sharks

An adult male
and female shark
meet and mate.

SHARK LIFE CYCLE
Some sharks have a life
cycle with these stages.

3

A black tip shark pup

2

A female lemon shark and pups

As soon as they are born, the
pups take care of themselves.
They have teeth and are
ready to hunt.

The female shark gives
birth to lots of pups at
the same time.

15

Deepsea anglerfish

The female anglerfish can open her mouth really wide to eat fish the same size as her.

Anglerfish live at the very bottom of deep oceans where it is very dark. The female has a long spine which comes out of her head. On the end is a ball that can glow like a light.

AMAZING FISH FACT

The male anglerfish becomes part of the female's body! When she eats, the food goes into the male's body too.

The female anglerfish uses her light to attract other fish—then she eats them!

The male anglerfish cannot feed himself. As soon as he is old enough, he has to find a female to live with.

The small male attaches himself to a female. They stay together for life. The male gets smaller and smaller.

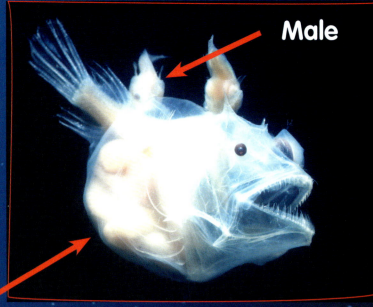

Male

Female

Light

When it is time to reproduce and lay eggs, the female already has her mate with her.

Salmon

Adult salmon live in the oceans. In the autumn, when it is time to mate and lay eggs, they have to swim back to the freshwater river where they were born.

A salmon who is ready to reproduce is called a spawner.

The salmon have a dangerous journey. They have to swim a long way, and they swim **upstream** which is very tiring.

AMAZING FISH FACT

The salmon have to leap up waterfalls and avoid predators such as grizzly bears.

Thousands of spawners gather in the same place.

Egg

Yolk sack

Alevin

When a female salmon reaches the spawning ground she makes four or five nests called redds. She lays about 1,000 eggs in each nest. Then a male fertilises the eggs.

The young salmon grow bigger and bigger. After about three years they are ready to swim out to sea.

The eggs hatch after four months. The small salmon are called alevins. They have an orange yolk sack which contains all the food they will need to grow.

Stickleback

Sticklebacks are tiny fish. They grow to just 5 cm long. Some sticklebacks live in saltwater close to the coast. Others live in freshwater ponds, lakes, and rivers.

Sticklebacks feed on tiny shellfish and the eggs of other small fish.

Between March and August the male stickleback changes colour to attract a mate

Nest

Then the male stickleback builds a nest from bits of plant. He does a zigzag dance in front of the nest to attract a female.

During the mating season, the underside of the male's body becomes a bright orange-red colour, his eyes turn blue, and silver scales appear on his back.

Male

Female

Lots of different females lay their eggs in the male's nest. Then he fertilises them.

Dogfish

Dogfish live in the ocean. They are a type of small shark. Adult dogfish are about one metre long. They spend most of their time on the seabed hunting for crabs, prawns and small fish.

Sharks have a skeleton made of cartilage. This is the bendy stuff your ears are made of.

This is a lesser spotted dogfish.

After mating, the female dogfish lays her eggs. Each egg is in its own little leathery case.

The female attaches the egg cases to pieces of seaweed so that they do not float away and get lost or damaged. The baby dogfish growing inside the case is called an embryo.

The embryo will stay in the case for about nine months. As it grows, it curls around the inside of its egg case.

By the time the baby dogfish is ready to hatch it will be about 10 cm long—twice as long as its egg case.

The egg cases are full of food for the embryo to eat.

Embryo

Egg case

AMAZING FISH FACT
Empty dogfish egg cases are sometimes washed up onto beaches. People call them mermaids' purses.

Seahorse

This very unusual looking fish has a horse-like head and a tail it can use to hold onto things. The seahorse can move each of its eyes separately—one can look forwards while the other looks backwards.

Before they mate, the male and female seahorses hold each other's tail, swim side-by-side, or swing around on a piece of seaweed together.

The seahorse's body is covered in armour made of hard, bony sections.

AMAZING FISH FACT
Seahorses can change colour to match their surroundings.

The male seahorse has a pouch on his tummy. The pouch is a bit like a pocket. The female lays her eggs inside the pouch and the male seahorse carries the eggs.

Most types of seahorse pair for life.

When the babies hatch, the male gives birth. He holds onto a piece of seaweed with his long tail. He rocks backwards and forwards until the babies pop out of his pouch. This can last for about two days.

Pouch

Baby seahorses

Lionfish

Lionfish live on coral reefs in warm seas.

Adult lionfish usually live alone, but when they are ready to mate they get together in groups. For three or four days, each male will try to get a female to notice him.

AMAZING FISH FACT
The lionfish's needle-like fins can give a predator a poisonous sting.

Sometimes the males will fight. They bite and ram each other with their spiky fins.

Fins

Adult lionfish are about 30 cm long.

When the male has found a partner, the two fish swim face to face and turn around in circles. They dance to the surface of the water.

On the surface of the water the female lays a ball of thousands of eggs. When the male has fertilised the eggs, the parents leave. After about three months the eggs hatch.

After hatching, the baby lionfish sink to the seabed to hide away from predators, such as bigger fish.

Hammerhead shark

An adult hammerhead is about 3-4 metres long.

Hammerhead sharks live in warm parts of the Pacific, Indian and Atlantic Oceans. They are strong swimmers and have been known to attack people!

The hammerhead shark has eyes and ears at each end of its wide head. Scientists believe having eyes like this might help the shark to see all around it when it is hunting.

Dorsal fin

Eye

The female hammerhead shark gives birth to about 20 to 40 pups at a time.

The pups are about 70 cm long when they are born. They look like small versions of the adults. The pups have to look after themselves as soon as they are born.

Hammerhead sharks eat fish and other sharks. Stingrays are their favourite food.

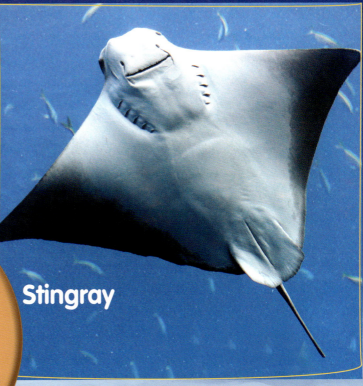

Stingray

AMAZING FISH FACT

Some sharks have several rows of very sharp teeth. When a tooth falls out, one from the row behind pushes forward to take its place.

That's amazing!

The male pearly jawfish looks after the female's eggs by keeping them in their mouths.

All fish big or small use their gills to breathe underwater. If humans want to spend time underwater studying fish life cycles and photographing them, we have to wear diving suits and breathe oxygen from a tank.

A female sunfish can lay 300 million eggs each year. Each egg is smaller than a full stop in this book.

AMAZING FISH FACT
The sunfish can grow to nearly four metres long, and can weigh up to 2,250 kg.

The river eel fish only breeds once in their life. They live in freshwater, but they migrate to the ocean to breed and lay their eggs.

As soon as sand tiger sharks are born, the largest baby sharks will kill and eat their baby brothers and sisters.

The ray's wings can measure 7 metres across.

Manta rays are huge plankton-eating fish with fins that look like wings. They swim by flapping their wings. The female manta ray gives birth to one or two babies each year.

Glossary

camouflage – colours, marks or a shape that hides an animal from its predators, and the animals it hunts.

coral reefs – underwater places that look rocky but are actually made from the bodies of coral animals called polyps. The polyps have hard skeletons that join together. When a polyp dies, its skeleton stays as part of the reef, so the reefs gets bigger and bigger.

freshwater – rainwater and the water in ponds and some rivers. It is not salty.

gills – breathing organs (parts of the body) in animals that live in water.

mate – when a male and female animal meet to have babies.

oxygen – a gas that all animals need for life.

plankton – tiny animals and plants that live in oceans and lakes. They are so small you need a microscope to see them.

predators – animals which hunt and kill other animals for food.

reproduce – to have babies.

saltwater – water with salt in it. The oceans and some lakes are saltwater.

scales – small, overlapping sections of hard skin that cover the bodies of fish.

sea anemones – an ocean animal with stinging tentacles—it looks like a plant!

stages – different times of an animal's life when the animal changes.

swamps – very wet areas with lots of water plants.

upstream – the opposite direction to the flow of water in a river or stream.

Index

Picture credits

Shutterstock. 1: Rich Carey. 2-3: Joe Belanger. 4-5: Nomad_Soul, Chonlasub Woravichan, HelloRF Zcool, Wildestanimal. 6-7: Podoinaya Elena, Stockphoto-graf, 3DMI, Rich Carey. 8-9: Andy Deitsch, Krysztof Odziomek, Simagart, Johannes Kornelius, Williamn Cushman. 10-11: Fedbull, Andrew Burgess, Andrey Armyagov, Vladmior Wrangei. 12-13: Rich Carey, Brandelet. 14-15: RW Brooks, YUSRAN ABDUL RAHMAN, Francisco Caravan, Brad Bowins. 16-17: Neil Bromhall. 18-19: Galyna Andrushko, Bierchen, Timothy Yue. 20-21: ABS Natural History, Rudmer Zwerver. 22-23: Boris Pamikov, IrinaK, Andrea Izzotti, JoLin. 24-25: CReativemarc, S. Rohrlach, Nicole Griffin Ward, Guido Montaldo, Studio 37, Floridan, Kristina Vackova, Rose3663. 26-27: Vision Dive, Richard Whitcombe, Brent Barnes, Agarianna76. 28-29: Nicolasvoisin44, wildestanimal, starryvoyage, Vicki L. Miller. 30-31: Fine Art Photos, Feathercollector, Rostislav Stefanek, MP cz, Tom F Cannon.

Every effort has been made to trace the copyright holders, and we apologize in advance for any unintentional omissions. We would be pleased to insert the appropriate acknowledgements in any subsequent edition of this publication.